Business as Usual

by Jean Battlo

Single copies of plays are sold for reading purposes only. The copying or duplicating of a play, or any part of play, by hand or by any other process, is an infringement of the copyright. Such infringement will be vigorously prosecuted.

Baker's Plays
7611 Sunset Blvd.
Los Angeles, CA 90042
bakersplays.com

NOTICE

This book is offered for sale at the price quoted only on the understanding that, if any additional copies of the whole or any part are necessary for its production, such additional copies will be purchased. The attention of all purchasers is directed to the following: this work is fully protected under the copyright laws of the United States of America, the British Commonwealth, including Canada, and all other countries of the Copyright Union. Violations of the Copyright Law are punishable by fine or imprisonment, or both. The copying or duplication of this work or any part of this work, by hand or by any process, is an infringement of the copyright and will be vigorously prosecuted.

This play may not be produced by amateurs or professionals for public or private performance without first submitting application for performing rights. Royalties are due on all performances whether for charity or gain, or whether admission is charged or not. Since performance of this play without the payment of the royalty fee renders anybody participating liable to severe penalties imposed by the law, anybody acting in this play should be sure, before doing so, that the royalty fee has been paid. Professional rights, reading rights, radio broadcasting, television and all mechanical rights, etc. are strictly reserved. Application for performing rights should be made directly to BAKER'S PLAYS.

No one shall commit or authorize any act or omission by which the copyright of, or the right to copyright, this play may be impaired. No one shall make any changes in this play for the purpose of production.

Publication of this play does not imply availability for performance. Both amateurs and professionals considering a production are strongly advised in their own interest to apply to Baker's Plays for written permission before starting rehearsals, advertising, or booking a theatre.

Whenever the play is produced, the author's name must be carried in all publicity, advertising and programs. Also, the following notice must appear on all printed programs, "Produced by special arrangement with Baker's Plays."

Licensing fees for BUSINESS AS USUAL is based on a per performance rate and payable one week in advance of the production.

Please consult the Baker's Plays website at www.bakersplays.com or our current print catalogue for up to date licensing fee information.

Copyright © 2010 by Jean Battlo
Made in U.S.A.
All rights reserved.

BUSINESS AS USUAL
ISBN **978-0-87440-238-4**
#2053-B

CHARACTERS

(in order of appearance)

GRAN – 76, Tom's mother, with the "grits" to overcome obstacles.

BESS WOOLWINE – 47, Tom's wife, cautious.

TOM WOOLWINE – 55, unemployed coal miner, proud but desperate family provider.

MAGGIE WOOLWINE – 18, the Woolwines' intelligent daughter, struggling to cope.

JOEY WOOLWINE – 21 year-old son, sharp, witty, torn between staying in economically ruined town or following his wife's demand to leave.

ANNABEL TOLLIVER – 42, the "body."

TONI – 28, the unexpected visitor.

BILL PRICE – 63, the mayor of Kimball, West Virginia.

PLACE

The economically defunct coal mining town of Kimball, West Virginia.

TIME

May, 1998; the last standing #6 mine has just closed.

ACT ONE

Scene One

(SETTING: A single set, divided into three parts. The largest space is the family room, stage right, with a partial wall. From the family room, a door leads to the kitchen, stage left, with a screen door at the end of the kitchen that opens onto a small porch area where Gran's rocker sits throughout the play.)

(*Set design and dimensions are at the end of the text.)

*(AT RISE: In the kitchen, **GRAN** and **BESS** are cooking, setting the table and singing hymns as **TOM**, dressed in camouflage coat and hat and sipping a beer, enters through the family room, listens to the singing a moment.)*

GRAN/BESS. *(singing)* "Farther along, we'll know all about it. Farther along we'll understand why. Cheer up my brothers! Live in the sunshine. We'll understand it all, by and by."

*(They hum as **BESS** gets biscuits from the oven; **GRAN** arranges forsythia stems in a Mason jar on table as **TOM** enters the kitchen.)*

TOM. *(leans against the refrigerator, mocks, sings)* Yeah, we're going to understand it all – all by and byyyyyeeeee.

*(**GRAN** and **BESS** turn to look as he tilts back on his heels and finishes off the can; he looks at them. Turns the can upside down as proof it is empty. He then flings it far stage left toward the trash can and misses.)*

GRAN. *(sarcasm)* Looks like our hunter's home from the hills.

TOM. Looks like, *(crosses left, picks up can and puts it in trash)* I'm just hoping you didn't put any hope on this hunter because I didn't hit anything on the mountain but the mountain.

BESS. And we had our hearts set on owl steak.

(BESS kisses him as she takes his baseball hat off, and hangs it on one of the hooks by the screen door.)

Sit down and don't act the fool.

(gives him a push into a chair)

GRAN. *(disguising concern)* We're having chicken. *(beat)* I shot it myself.

TOM. *(laughs with BESS as GRAN messes with forsythia)* You have aim, Mama. And what are you fixing there, a dry twig soup?

GRAN. You know I always force forsythia into blooming, *(goes to stove to stir beans)* Tom. Have you been drinking?

TOM. Me? Not so you'd notice. *(savoring memory)* But that was sure one fine little ol' beer while it lasted.

GRAN. Doesn't look like it lasted all that long.

TOM. *(more serious)* Whatever does, Mama? Sorrow. Woe.

BESS. You're acting funny.

(GRAN and BESS are in constant motion, carrying plates and food to the table.)

TOM. Strange, Bess. You have to watch language nowadays. Better strange than funny.

BESS. *(growing concerned)* Tom, be serious?

TOM. I will, if you won't. You've never been a nagger and believe me, this is not a good day to start.

GRAN. Why would she nag? Just because you spent the last family dollar ninety-eight for a beer?

TOM. You either, Mama. Let's just all lighten up. Actually, if you give it a little thought, a beer is about as sound an investment a Woolwine can afford to make right now.

BESS. We're talking investments now.

TOM. You never know. You can't tell what sort of pig you have in the poke 'til you get the poke home.

GRAN. *(looks at* **BESS***)* I think he had bourbon in that beer.

TOM. *(joking, but touchy)* And I might point out we have more than a dollar ninety-eight.

GRAN. And I might point out you invested in more than one beer.

TOM. *(sits, lifts glass)* I'd drink to that. If I had a drink. *(stops joking)* Let's just eat.

*(***GRAN** *and* **BESS** *sit.)*

Pass the chicken.

(grabs a leg, starts to take a bite)

BESS. I was thinking we might pray first.

*(***TOM** *abruptly drops the leg, folds his hands and start the prayer;* **GRAN** *and* **BESS***, caught off guard, quickly bow their heads.)*

TOM. Gracious, Father! *(opens one eye to see if* **BESS** *is upset)* We want to thank you for what you give – the dollar ninety-eight Mama mentioned...

*(***GRAN** *opens one eye, gives him a warning look.)*

...and for our health of course, and for each other...

*(***MAGGIE** *sneaks hurriedly on and sits at the table.)*

...and I even thank you for the tardy daughter who has been told time and again...

*(***MAGGIE** *open her eyes and looks at* **TOM.***)*

...by her mother NOT to be late for this family's dinner, and for all this, we praise you. Amen.

MAGGIE. That's funny, Dad.

BESS. *(passing food around, irritated)* Strange, Maggie, he wants to be called strange. And Tom, I won't have that kind of joking at prayer. I take it you didn't get the job.

TOM. You take it right.

BESS. I knew it. I just knew it, I got up this morning and I had a funny feeling.

GRAN. Could have been gas, Bessie-girl.

BESS. *(realizing they are trying to make it easier for* **TOM***)* Well, it wasn't the last job in the world.

TOM. It just about was. And, for sure, it was the last job in West Virginia. And so, I add

(He drops his biscuit and rushes back into prayer. **ALL** *bow their heads, not knowing if he's serious.)*

Gracious Father, I have to tell you, I'm having a little problem understanding why you couldn't at least give me a little demolition job for a couple of days so I could make a couple of hundred to tide us over, but you do work in mysterious ways –

BESS. Tom Woolwine! That is entirely enough!

TOM. I'm sorry. You're right. No need to take it out on God. It's just that we need that money more than Gran needs All-Bran.

*(***ALL*** laugh.)*

GRAN. You should go so good.

TOM. *(appeasing* **BESS***)* You know, hons, if we don't joke, we get serious. And don't go looking all sad. We'll make it. Farther along.

MAGGIE. Dad, I did think this one job was a sure thing for you.

TOM. So did I. And so did about sixty other guys. The only sure thing is there's no sure thing left around here.

MAGGIE. That's a bummer. I was counting on a little help with tuition.

BESS. Maggie.

MAGGIE. I'm sorry, that got out before I thought.

TOM. It's all right. You have a right to be disappointed.

MAGGIE. I didn't mean it like that. I can start college later.

TOM. Ha. By the time you start college, you'll have forgotten how to read and write.

BESS. *(***MAGGIE*** laughs; to* **MAGGIE***)* You didn't get the job at the Pizza Inn?

MAGGIE. They wanted to hire me. But they're closing the first of the month.

TOM. Great! Works for me. Now the town won't be all cluttered with businesses.

BESS. Let's stay hopeful.

TOM. And why not? With Kroger gone and Murphy's closing, our town has this real neat street of completely boarded up buildings.

MAGGIE. Another West Virginia first, "ghost malls."

BESS. You're going to be just like him, Maggie.

GRAN. *(pensive)* I remember Ben Green saying Kroger would never close.

TOM. He had to think that. He worked there. *(beat)* A man can't let himself believe his work will end.

BESS. You'll find something else. You've had these odd jobs now and again. We're okay.

TOM. I remember saying U.S. Steel would never leave Gary. A man believes what he has to.

(**JOEY** *enters family room, crosses to kitchen.*)

GRAN. That hurt sure enough, but it was the strikes that helped cause it, son.

JOEY. So, a man should just take anything they throw at him, huh, Gran?

GRAN. Didn't say that.

TOM. Strikes didn't close the mines. Nor technology. That's what they want us to think.

JOEY. It was big business. Other countries buying our little county. Ecologists.

MAGGIE. Environment matters, Joey!

JOEY. I can't eat trees, Maggie! And my wife would like a new dress every couple of years or so.

TOM. U.S. Steel leaving was the death blow.

JOEY. Like it matters. Thing is, everyone with the sense God gave a corncob left the coal fields.

GRAN. Are you going somewhere, Joey?

JOEY. No, Gran, I ain't going nowhere!

BESS. You watch how you speak to Gran, boy!

JOEY. I'm sorry, Gran.

GRAN. It's just the times. Have something to eat?

JOEY. Ha, eat. The family solution. I'm not hungry. I'm just here to talk.

TOM. Well, watch what you say. I don't like leaving-talk, son.

JOEY. I'm just saying.

TOM. Well, don't be saying that at this table. Don't talk about leaving in front of me.

JOEY. *(suppressing anger)* Let it go, Dad.

TOM. We're just hitting hard times. I know you wanted that job today, son. It was a little setback.

JOEY. Setback! We're out of work for years and you call that a little setback!

TOM. Yeah, that's what I call it. What? A little trouble and you're running off like your brothers did?

JOEY. I'm not leaving.

TOM. I'm glad to hear it, 'cause it rubs a man a little raw raising six kids and only having two left in sight. That makes a man edgy.

JOEY. I *am* here, so, don't start. I'm here in spite of Diane threatening to leave me if I don't leave here.

MAGGIE. She's just upset.

BESS. I'll talk to her.

JOEY. She's not upset, Mom. She's desperate, and embarrassed.

GRAN. Embarrassed? How? Nothing is your all's fault.

JOEY. No, but all our friends are gone. They wouldn't take welfare, either, so they went after work.

TOM. Just like your brothers.

JOEY. Believe me, it's not a good day to talk to me about my brothers and sister that got out of West Virginia.

TOM. Now I can't talk about my kids leaving.

(Each interrupts the others' statements.)

JOEY. Those kids are working, Dad. They have jobs.

TOM. Jobs? You call making brassieres work?

JOEY. Matter of fact, yes, I do! I call making bras work when you get a paycheck twice a month

TOM. We've been a mining family since Day-One of creation

JOEY. I call it work when you can go out and buy anything you want –

TOM. And you're telling me my grown sons making bras in Danville, Virginia are working?

JOEY. – Yes, sir, when a man can buy a steak, a gallon of Jack Daniels or jalapeno potato chips and dip, yes, I do!

GRAN. *(stops the tirade)* Bessie, you raised a son that thinks jalapeno potato chips is food.

BESS. What interests me more is his relationship with Mr. Daniels.

JOEY. I'm not joking.

MAGGIE. *(protective of parents)* Obvious.

BESS. It's not like you to get this discouraged.

TOM. Exactly. We've made it this far.

JOEY. Barely. You know it's been three years since I've had a steady job.

BESS. Give it time, son.

JOEY. I don't feel right. You didn't raise me like that…I don't feel like a real person, I get up mornings and just sit there with a emptying cup of coffee and a full day of time.

TOM. It does against the grain.

JOEY. It's doing damage real deep in me, Dad.

TOM. I feel every bit of that. But like I said, we're making it.

JOEY. Like I said, barely.

TOM. *(Finally loses control. Slams table.)* Barely, bareass! *(jumps up, almost topples chair)*

BESS. Thomas Lloyd!

TOM. I can't help it. I'm not listening to this nonsense.

JOEY. I was only saying –

TOM. Home! Is there anyone living in the world nowadays who remembers what home is? A man doesn't just up and leave home.

JOEY. But when it's necessary –

TOM. Necessary-schmecessary! You're eating a whole lot better than beans and greens, so don't hand me this jalapeno and Jack Daniels business.

BESS. Calm down, Tom. And Joey, it's not like you to whine.

JOEY. I'm not whining. And it's not like he says, and that's why he's so upset. Dad, you know where I'm coming from.

(All are silenced a moment; continues reluctantly.)

Somebody of us has got to say this sooner or later. *(beat)* We can't make it here anymore.

TOM. *(Lifts chicken leg: as Macbeth)* Is this a chicken leg I see before me?

JOEY. From a special commodity program, Dad. It's almost charity.

TOM. Don't say that. I paid for this.

JOEY. Thirteen dollars for a fifty-dollar "surprise" box from the government. It's charity! And I earn my living. The state's dying. Coal is over. We can't live on dollars and cents.

*(Despondent, **TOM** sits down.)*

MAGGIE. It'll get better. There's talk.

JOEY. And you believe it. There's been talk all our lives, and there's still nothing here!

TOM. What do you mean by "nothing?"

JOEY. Nothing as in nothing. Nada. Zero We're on empty, like bottomed out. Do you know if Diane and I want to see a movie, we have to drive fifty miles?

TOM. So you want to leave home for the movies?

JOEY. It's not important to you, but it is to me.

TOM. Then drive fifty miles and see movies.

JOEY. Even Mercer County doesn't get them all. It took over two months for *Scream* to get to the mall cinemas.

TOM. You're spoiling my supper over *Scream*?

JOEY. Dad, don't get mad. It's not fair. I stayed for you. I love it here, but I have to get a life.

TOM. I hear Boyd Hendrick may be hiring help to build a fence.

JOEY. And when we heard they might build a sewing factory at Hemphill, six hundred people showed up for those eleven jobs.

(All sit in silent thought a moment.)

If Boyd hires, what can he pay, twenty bucks? Hell, a box of cereal costs that much. There's just nothing left.

GRAN. But the people. The people are still here. Like always.

JOEY. I hear you, Gran, and believe me, I don't like what I'm saying,

GRAN. I know. But you have to believe. It's not over. Everything is not all gone.

MAGGIE. Everyone's leaving.

GRAN. Never believe it. We people were here before there was a West Virginia, and you can bet your by-gollys we'll be here if there's no state left!

MAGGIE. You go, girl.

GRAN. You listen up. Our first people came to the hills, married up with others, Indians or whatevers. Why you look real close at any Collins or Lester or Jackson and you can still see Indian in their eyes.

JOEY. History won't wok. This is here, now. Used-to-be is not the point right now.

GRAN. Used-to-be is always the point. 'Cause we're the stuff of those same hard-timers. That same, fine, full pioneer blood runs in your veins right now. The people is all that ever matters. People is all there ever was or will be.

BESS. But, Gran, the point is they can't find work.

GRAN. What you can't find, you make. Talking about heritage here. Talking about clearing wilderness...

MAGGIE. Joey can't eat wilderness.

GRAN. *(no pause)* ...talking about gouging out boulders, tilling rocky fields till they yield. Talking about looking it all in the face and making a life out of it.

JOEY. I respect that. But the mines are as over as Bob Dole.

GRAN. You hear me, boy! I'm talking about before a mine was a gleam in an operators eye. Talking about doing with what you got.

JOEY. But are you hearing me? I'm a third generation miner, and we're closed.

GRAN. You're just young. And you suffer from it. Life's just a seesaw, all up and down, you get used to it. What goes up has got to come down and vicey-versey. Now, maybe mines'll come back. Maybe not.

MAGGIE. Hate to admit it, but my money's on – NOT.

GRAN. You just keep your eye on that Johnny Jay Rockefeller and see what's up his sleeve. But regardless, us people will be here. Yes, sir, and you'd better believe it! *(All laugh but* **GRAN**.*)*

TOM. *(amused)* Think so. Mama?

GRAN. Know so! Because when Gabriel comes to these West-by-God-Virginia hills to blow his horn, us people will be right here tap dancing to the tunes o' glory.

ALL. Here, here, Gran!

JOEY. Here, here, here, Gran, but one thing? How?

GRAN. You ask like its dirty clothes to hang on a line but happens I've been thinking. And I've thought how we can make money right here at home.

TOM. Come on, Mama. We've tried everything legal.

GRAN. Talking about us going into business for ourselves.

MAGGIE. Yo, Gran, you are the family treasure. With all the big companies going bust, us pissant peasants are going to open a new one. Excuse me.

GRAN. Indeedy. And watch that mouth. I told your father not to get HBO.

BESS. *(smiles)* She didn't learn "pissant peasant" on TV. And we don't get HBO.

GRAN. Don't tell me. Did I see her watching a show the other night where they're in bed and the husband comes hollering at the wife because it's not him in bed with her?

MAGGIE. *(laughs)* Just Americas Funniest Home Videos, Gran. Regular Sunday night TV.

GRAN. You're not on regular TV, so watch that mouth. Now, about this family business.

TOM. You're half-serious. Don't get some fool notion because we can't open when everyone is closing.

GRAN. *(triumphant)* Everything ain't closing.

JOEY. Well, there's no Tiffany's in Kimball.

MAGGIE. We could open up and sell diamonds and emeralds right here in downtown, Kimball, West Virginia. No competition.

(All laugh but **GRAN.***)*

TOM. And who wouldn't want to drive to McDowell County just for the road experience?

JOEY. Yeah. Ha ha, these roads ride like Disney World.

TOM. Ha, there's a pothole near Northfork where it dips down so it'd take a crane to lift you up out of it. *(more laughter)*

GRAN. I am whole, teetotalling serious here.

TOM. I think you are. You really have an idea, Mama?

GRAN. I do. I put on my good ol' West Virginia – native-grit-and-go-get-it thinking cap on.

JOEY. That and about $100,000 New York dollars should get us started.

GRAN. Joey, I don't just talk to break wind.

JOEY. Sorry. It's hard to take serious. No one can buy much around here anyway.

GRAN. Some things they have to.

MAGGIE. You mean, we're going to sell toilet paper? *(laughter)*

GRAN. *(commandingly)* GET SERIOUS. Now. All businesses are not closed. Think about it. What's not closing? What never closes? What goes on, business as usual? What's got a nice building, usually with white columns still standing in McDowell County?

BESS. I can't think of anything. What are you talking about, Gran?

GRAN. Woodlawn Cemetery. Business as usual.

MAGGIE. Woodlawn? You want us to start burying people in the back yard?

GRAN. Don't talk the fool. I mean Woodlawn, and its tributaries.

TOM. Tributaries? What's a tributary to a cemetery?

GRAN. *(smiles, lifts the jar of forsythia twigs)* Fanning Funeral Home. Douglas Funeral Home. Business as usual at every undertaker for a hundred mile radius.

Scene Two

(The following morning. **JOEY** *sits on the sofa in the family room. In the kitchen,* **BESS** *pours them both a cup of coffee and carries it to him, sits beside him.)*

BESS. Undertakers!

JOEY. Morticians! The Addams Family of West Virginia.

BESS. Can you believe it?

JOEY. It's what Gran said and I think she meant it.

BESS. The very suggestion boggled my mind.

JOEY. Me, too. Ha, Gran thinks we Woolwines can do anything.

BESS. This is too crazy even for us to consider. You do know its crazy, don't you, Joey?

JOEY. Absolutely. But the funny and strange thing is, I believe Dad's giving it real thought.

BESS. He is not! *(rapid rationalization; one sentence)* Don't let him fool you, Tom respects Gran and doesn't like to disagree with her, but I am absolutely sure he would never give something like this serious thought. *(adds, without a pause)* You don't think he's giving this serious thought, do you, Joey?

JOEY. What I think is you're trying to convince yourself.

BESS. Believe me, someone has to do it.

JOEY. I'm sure he'll decide against it, but it is steeping in his brain.

BESS. You're wrong. *(pauses, sips coffee)* What do you think Maggie thinks?

JOEY. It's hard enough to know what normal people think, much less Maggie.

BESS. Don't be the big brother, now. Seriously.

JOEY. She's Daddy's girl. If Dad says the moon is margarine, Maggie tries butter up on moonshine. So I guess it comes down to what Dad decides.

BESS. Decides? You make it sound like it's a possible decision. Why, he's so sensible, we're silly to even speculate. Why he'll come in laughing about the whole thing.

JOEY. I hope so.

BESS. I know so.

JOEY. Diane's always had reservations about this family. I just hope she never even hears that it was mentioned.

BESS. Is your wife all that bothers you? I'd rather you were more upset. You are not as upset as I'd like you to be, Joey.

JOEY. I'm upset, I'm upset. It's just when Gran gets hold of an idea, she hops on it like a horse and rides it till you think it's possible.

BESS. Now *you're* scaring me.

(**TOM** *enters reading a book on ancient Egypt with a mummy on the cover; a large hook is visible in his back pocket.*)

JOEY. Not to worry, Mom, I'm the rational one.

BESS. I pray to that effect. Tom, what are you reading?

TOM. I'm not actually reading this. Joey, could you describe a clyster?

JOEY. Someone who tries to trick you.

BESS. *(increasingly agitated)* He did not say shyster, and I remember clysters from history class. Tom, what are you reading?

TOM. Lighten up, Bessie. It's just a book. And I'm not reading it.

BESS. Tom! What! Is! The book! About?

TOM. Okay, all right, for crying out loud, Egyptians! Is there a law against reading Egyptian history?

JOEY. See, Mom, you're upset, and he's just doing his every-early morning-ancient-Egyptian history reading.

BESS. I knew it! I just knew it! Joey, I said I couldn't handle your humor right now, and Tom, what have you got to do with Egyptians?

TOM. I am not having to-do with Egyptians, Bess.

JOEY. You better start laughing, Mom.

TOM. It's just that Mama got me curious.

BESS. Curious. Here's a word, "curious."

TOM. Yeah. *(points to book)* Now, in here it says they used the clyster-thing to jerk entrails out of the cadaver before –

BESS. Oh, Lord, no!

TOM. Oh, yes. *(shoves the book toward her)* Says so. There's a picture.

BESS. *(shoves book away)* Don't bring that near me, **TOM.** What are you thinking?

TOM. I am not thinking!

JOEY. You are so right.

TOM. Cut it, Joey. It's just that last night's talk got me wondering.

BESS. You cannot be serious.

TOM. Serious? Oh, ha ha, I see. You think I'm thinking- No, no. *(absentmindedly pulls a hook out of his pocket)*

BESS. If you are not thinking about it, why are you reading up on it?

TOM. I don't call this "reading up" on it.

JOEY. Have you got a hook there, Dad?

BESS. Dear Lord, he has a hook. A clyster.

TOM. No such thing. Earth to Bess, for crying out loud. Besides, they don't use clysters now.

BESS. Is this a real conversation?

TOM. It is not, I just think it odd that death and dying are everyday things and we don't know beans about embalming.

JOEY. Things you wanted to know about embalming but were too alive to ask.

TOM. Don't you find it odd we don't know more about common things?

*(**GRAN** enters, listens silently.)*

BESS. I can't believe what I'm hearing.

TOM. You're not hearing anything. I'm talking history. We don't do things like the Egyptians, anymore.

JOEY. I, for one, have abandoned all Egyptian habits.

TOM. Here's something interesting. *(indicates book)* Seems they put a body in some sort of vat, forty or seventy days, depending on your wealth.

JOEY. I'll need about an eighty-day soak.

BESS. I asked you not to joke.

TOM. The bottom line is, if an idiot like Fred Johnson can do it, anyone can.

BESS. And that leads us where?

TOM. It leads us nowhere.

JOEY. And once again, you are so right.

TOM. You're getting on my nerves, son.

BESS. If you're just talking history, why is he getting on your nerves?

TOM. Okay, you want to hear it. Because I've given it some thought.

GRAN. *(stands close to* **TOM***)* That's my boy! Just listen it out, Bessie. It's the one West Virginia business that's still business as usual. I mean to use it myself one day.

BESS. Gran, you can't just decide to go into undertaking and just go out and hang up a shingle.

GRAN. You should be able to. That's what pioneering is about, finding new territory and then going out to master it.

JOEY. Tilling the fields, clearing the wilderness –

BESS. *(ignoring* **JOEY***)* Gran, he knows nothing about undertaking!

GRAN. So? What did the Wrights know about flying till they went out and flew?

JOEY. Manning the trenches, flying the planes –

GRAN. *(continues)* And did Adam know about undertaking when Eve passed, or vicey versey? Good Book's not always clear. So there, Day-One, they had a dead beloved, so they just fixed her up and buried her.

JOEY. *(growing serious)* Hey, Gran, things aren't that simple now, Gran.

GRAN. Ought to be. That's what's wrong with now. Things ought to be that simple. Take the American Revolution.

JOEY. Obvious argument.

GRAN. When this country was getting born with the bodies lying here, there and everywhere, where you figure those forefathers and soldiers got an undertaker?

JOEY. A rational question.

TOM. *(reading)* Listen… "First they draw the brain out through the nostril…"

BESS. *(screams)* NO! Tom, don't read that.

TOM. Sorry. I got carried away.

JOEY. *(under his breath)* Little men in white are going to carry us all away.

BESS. Tom, I want the truth. What are you thinking?

GRAN. He's thinking we might start a highly successful West Virginia business!

BESS. No, he's not.

GRAN. It's business, like any other. Time was when folks did their neighbors out of friendship. Though now, it's a going business.

BESS. Then why not try mid-wiving and catch life at the other end?

TOM. It can be simple. Take some things out of the body. Wax it up a bit.

BESS. What do you use? Johnson's Wax? Rain Dance?

TOM. Not that kind of wax. I know I don't know all the details.

GRAN. But he can learn. It's mountain-ingenuity striking again.

BESS. Mountain madness! You can't just open a funeral home and embalm.

GRAN. Used to be people did just that. Went to a friends and did it. Now, they have classes at Bluefield State to tell you how to breathe when birthing babies.

BESS. Don't talk him into this, Gran. It's against the law. You have to have a degree, a license.

TOM. We stayed up talking about it. We know there'll be problems, obstacles.

BESS. You make it sound like getting a Dairy Queen franchise.

TOM. We'll start slow.

BESS. I see. Just a body or two, no one will notice.

TOM. We've thought of everything. We'll just tell our friends here. And who else cares what's going on in southern West Virginia? We're economically deprived. Dying to live, and nobody in Charleston gives a whistle, you think they're going to care who opens a funeral home here if we keep quiet? When was the last time Underwood or Clinton called Kimball up to see how we were doing down here'?

JOEY. Now, that's gospel! Washington doesn't know there's a West Virginia, and Charleston doesn't think they can get here from there.

TOM. Given the roads, you almost can't. *(laughter)* What have we got here, Bess? Five-, six-hundred people. All in it together. Half of us are broke and all hoping, helping each other as best we can. So, if we tell friends were starting a business they'll want to help.

JOEY. But we won't ask them to just up and die for us?

BESS. What do you think Fred Johnson will do when you run out and bury people for cut-rate?

GRAN. Won't matter. People stay mad about his prices.

TOM. *(trying to convince them and himself)* And when people know we're just trying to work and stay home and when they realize we're not after big profits off their sorrow and that our low prices will help them, too, they'll come running…*(beat)* Well, maybe not running.

GRAN. There you go. Of course, there's still little glitches.

JOEY. Like, for instance, will folks mind having their loved ones toted in a Ford pickup instead of a fancy hearse?

GRAN. Happens that's what folks won't mind when they learn what they'll save.

BESS. What about the mayor? What will Bill Price say?

TOM. I figure Bill will give us an honorary plaque, considering what it cost him to put Alice away, No, seriously, Bill will understand this. After all, he didn't get to be mayor of Kimball without brains.

GRAN. Tom will explain it to him.

BESS. What? That a fairy came by and zap! He's a mortician?

TOM. Look. We're desperate. People understand that. With Stevens Clinic closed, you're lucky if you can die here, much less get buried. *(pause)* Think about it, Bess. This is our first "maybe" in a long, long time.

BESS. But this *is*… *(beat) desperate.*

TOM. I have to do something. Joey and Diane are afraid to have kids because they can't afford them. That's as wrong as life gets. Maggie's the smartest one we've had, and we don't have a semester's tuition for her.

BESS. But it's illegal, Tom.

TOM. And as soon as we get a little money from the first body, first thing we do is start legalizing. We send Joey to school with the first dollar. I figure we can make six-seven thousand at first.

BESS. No. Now, I'm not agreeing, but if we ever should do something like this, we wouldn't charge grieving people much. They rob you to death over funerals.

JOEY. We'll have fair prices. But we have to have a profit. We could charge maybe half of the other undertakers do and still do all right. *(calculating)* Of course, I don't know what overhead is like.

GRAN. What 'overhead'? The rich just sucked the living to death and then went after the dead. Overhead, posh and piddle. All you do is wash it, ready it, and put it in a pine box.

JOEY. We'll need more information. It's not hooks and vats now. All I know is you get the blood out.

TOM. Exactly. Just puncture it?

JOEY. But what kind of equipment will we need'?

TOM. We can't be investing in fancy equipment before we have a real...case.

JOEY. I guess not. You guess there's some sort of drill?

BESS. Don't talk this talk. It sounds awful.

JOEY. There's probably no scenic route to embalming, Mom. I am wondering if the sheriff and Mayor Price will let us try this, though. It is sort of awesome.

TOM. Believe me. We get Dollar-One and send you to classes.

BESS. I doubt Bluefield State has an Undertaking 101 class.

TOM. There you go. Raining on parades. We'll work out all the little "illegals."

BESS. I just hope the law doesn't execute people over these "little illegals."

JOEY. It is starting to feel possible. We could have a highly successful West Virginia business right here at home.

BESS. At home! Don't even say it. I can't believe I'm sitting here talking like this.

MAGGIE. *(runs on, out of breath)* Listen, listen, everyone listen. It's incredible!

BESS. What in the world's happened?

MAGGIE. You're not going to believe me.

GRAN. Get a hold, girl, you're coming undone.

MAGGIE. Well, just wait till you hear –

TOM. Hear what'! You're babbling.

MAGGIE. *(continues)* – You'll have a conniption-fit. You'll think this is God's will, for sure.

BESS. *(firmly)* Maggie, make sense!

MAGGIE. *(blurts)* Annabel Tolliver is what I'm telling you.

BESS. What about Annabel? Is she drunk on the street again?

MAGGIE. Annabel just dropped dead at the Powhatan Tavern!

(All react.)

JOEY. Dead? Are you sure?

MAGGIE. I'm sure. I couldn't wait to tell you!

BESS. You check that attitude, young lady, and show respect! Annabel may have been a drunk, but the Tollivers are our friends.

MAGGIE. I'm sorry as can be, but not surprised. It must have taken a legion of angels to keep her liver living.

TOM. Show respect, like you were told. *(beat)* I worked twenty years in the mines with Ed Tolliver.

MAGGIE. That's just it, Dad. They're friends. And I told her brother, Jamey, that we were trying to start up in the business, don't you all see?

JOEY. See what?

MAGGIE. We'll get Annabel! Now, if that's not providence, I don't know what is. We get the idea one night, and the next morning, bam! We get a body.

BESS. I doubt I'm ever going to see it that way.

TOM. Our "maybe," Bess.

GRAN. You have to admit, it's a pondering thing to have happen right now.

BESS. Maybe. May be.

(lights down)

Scene Three

*(**BESS** and **GRAN** are folding laundry in the kitchen. **TOM** and **JOEY** enter from the back of the theater, clumsily carrying **ANNABEL**, draped in a sheet. The business with the body begins: they drop her legs, struggle with her in various positions, etc. Their increasing nervousness builds climatically throughout the scene as the cold reality of gradually dawns on them.)*

JOEY. *(dropping and quickly retrieving a leg)* Gee whiz, she's heavy.

TOM. Hold her! Of course she's heavy, she's dead.

*(**ANNABEL**'s arms flop out of the sheet.)*

JOEY. What? Do you gain weight dying?

TOM. Stay focused. Matter of fact, I reckon you gain weight or something. You know, dead weight.

JOEY. You can't add flesh when you're dead, for crying out loud.

TOM. *(arriving stage right; talk mainly to avoid thinking about what they are doing)* Yeah. Now you mention it, I read some bodies lose weight. People argue that proves there was a soul that left the body, so, less pounds.

*(**ANNABEL** begins to slide from his arms.)*

JOEY. Don't talk theology. I'm about to drop her.

TOM. No. No, you are not. This is Annabel. Hold her tighter.

JOEY. I couldn't hold her any tighter if she were Madonna!

TOM. Just hold her, Joey.

JOEY. I'm doing my best! We should have got a stretcher. Or a dolly.

TOM. *(looks around desperately)* I don't know where to lay her. I haven't thought that far ahead.

JOEY. That doesn't seem all that far ahead to me when I have a dead body in my arms.

TOM. Shut up and let me think. We'll need some sort of table. Now, you'll have to hold alone a minute.

JOEY. You're joking, I can't.

(*JOEY drops her legs.*)

TOM. You have to.

(*lifts* **ANNABEL** *into* **JOEY**'s *arms and tries to arrange her*)

She's here now, and this is what we have to do.

JOEY. (*struggling with the body*) What are you going to be doing?

TOM. I'm going in there and ask your mother for the kitchen table.

JOEY. I'd bet a two copies of Playboy, you don't get her kitchen table.

(**JOEY** *back steps to the arm of the couch and sits with* **ANNABEL** *on his lap.*)

(**TOM** *ignores* **JOEY** *and goes to kitchen. In this split scene,* **JOEY** *struggles with the body in the family room as* **TOM** *tries to coax* **BESS.**)

TOM. Now, Bess, let me begin by saying I understand perfectly if you have some reservations about this.

BESS. "Reservations" doesn't come near what I'm feeling.

(*Flips clothes – in the family room:* **JOEY** *tries to lift* **ANNABEL**, *but falls back on sofa with the body on lop of him.*)

GRAN. Whatever you're feeling now. stuff it. We have to do what we have to do. We already decided.

TOM. She's got that as right as can be. We've done it.

(**JOEY** *makes an effort to listen.*)

BESS. You have got that right! You have absolutely done it.

TOM. I wasn't finished. We've done it.

(**JOEY** *tries to gets up, falls back.*)

I have to keep Annabel on my mind.

JOEY. (*aside, not heard in kitchen*) I wish she was just only my mind.

BESS. I can't discuss it.

TOM. You know what would have made the difference? If you had seen Ed. Then this would seem right and proper, just us caring for friends in need.

(*JOEY continues to struggle with the body on top of him during the following dialogue.*)

BESS. You already talk like a mortician. Don't come slinging that bull in here.

(*JOEY succeeds in getting ANNABEL back up to the arm of the couch, holding her in place. He comes around to the front of her to try and get her in a firemen's carry.*)

TOM. I'm talking about being neighborly. Charitable.

BESS. You are not. This is a business now, so don't make it sound like a trip to Africa for the children.

TOM. The point is! It's done! And the Tollivers are happy about it.

BESS. Why do I not think of the Tollivers as "happy" this morning?

TOM. Bess, give me a break.

JOEY. Better yet, give me a break.

GRAN. He didn't mean happy "happy."

TOM. Yeah, right. I just meant it seemed to console them some that it's us instead of strangers. You know, friends doing Annabel.

(*JOEY has ANNABEL up on his back and is taking a few tentative steps. He looks like Quasimoto.*)

BESS. Doing Annabel?

TOM. (*losing it*) That's it! That's all I can take! I admit to saying the wrong words, but I don't need this extra grief.

BESS. And this is my fault, because?

TOM. I didn't say it's your fault. I just have more to think about than I can think about.

BESS. You should have thought of that before.

(*JOEY finally gets the body in balance and walks over near the door to eavesdrop.*)

TOM. Bessie, please! Please, please, please help!

BESS. I'm sorry. This is my personal best.

GRAN. There, there now. Of course it is. Tom, sit down and talk to her.

TOM. Talk about it? Now?

JOEY. *(taps his head against the wall)* Don't talk now.

BESS. That might help. I've been thinking such thoughts.

TOM. But could it wait? I mean, I am really, really busy.

BESS. Now you're a businessman, too busy to talk.

TOM. More fact than funny. This work is as immediate as work gets.

BESS. I'm not trying to be funny. I've been thinking. *(pause)* I don't think this is religious.

(**JOEY** *can't take the standing weight any more, and stands* **ANNABEL** *up against the wall facing her with his palm on her chest to hold her against the wall.*)

TOM. You don't think it's religious! You think God has something against dying –

GRAN. Get a grip, son.

TOM. – because if God is against dying we ought to tell folks because a lot of them are doing it unintentionally and would just as soon not!

BESS. We can't have a serious conversation if you carry on like this. And that kind of joke is what I mean about it not being religious.

(Exasperated, **JOEY** *turns suddenly and* **ANNABEL** *crumples to the ground; using his back, he grabs her and forces her back up. Once he has her pinned to the wall, he realizes he is touching her breasts and pulls away quickly. She falls forward again and he catches her.)*

I mean, where is this leading us? What are people saying in town?

TOM. I knew you'd say that. I told Joey you'd worry about what people say!

BESS. Well, excuse me! We don't go into the funeral business everyday. I can just hear Dave Jenkins. *(mimics male voice)* "Looks like 'stead of coal-digging, the Woolwines are grave-digging to get rich."

TOM. No one is saying any such thing.

(**JOEY** *puts his back against* **ANNABEL** *to hold her against the wall.*)

BESS. I think so. I've hit the nail on the head. Or drove the nail in the coffin, whatever.

GRAN. Bess, you're surprising me to no end. You had your say. We talked already.

BESS. But it's different when you're actually doing it. You sounded so desperate, you talked me into it.

TOM. So what changed? Maybe you hit the lottery last night and didn't tell us.

(**JOEY** *gets her arms over his shoulders ready to assume the fireman's position again.*)

BESS. Don't get angry with me. I just can't feel right.

TOM. *(surrendering)* I know. *(puts his arm around her)* Let's just have some coffee.

JOEY. Don't have coffee!

TOM. You'll see. It will be all right.

JOEY. It's all wrong.

BESS. I am trying.

TOM. I can see that. And this is hard on you. *(embraces her)*

JOEY. This is hard on her, Annabel.

BESS. There's just so much going on inside me.

TOM. All of us, hons.

GRAN. Death just awakens things we shouldn't have let go to sleep. Bess, you ought to be ashamed.

TOM. Mama!

BESS. Gran's right. I know you're struggling with this, Tom.

JOEY. He's struggling, Annabel.

TOM. That's true.

BESS. I just feel confused. Us doing this. The Tollivers grieving and us saying we're helping, but taking pay for it. And I'm adding to the problems.

TOM. If you do see that, then maybe we can get started.

BESS. Give me one more minute.

(**JOEY** *groans.*)

TOM. Okay. What?

BESS. I'm afraid it's eating at Joey. He's never even seen a dead body. Don't you think he's having trouble with this?

JOEY. He's having trouble with this.

(*Laboriously,* **JOEY** *returns to the couch with* **ANNABEL**. *He tips backwards over the arm of the couch, and she lands on him again.*)

TOM. Naw, Joey's on top of it!

JOEY. It's on top of Joey.

BESS. He acts like he's taking it in stride.

(*Lights down in the kitchen; in shadows the actors appear to continue to talk as the lights brighten in the family room.* **MAGGIE** *enters looks at* **ANNABEL**.)

MAGGIE. Is that her?

JOEY. No, Maggie, it's Meg Ryan. She wanted to tour the coal fields incognito.

MAGGIE. You don't have to be so smart.

JOEY. Then don't be dumb. Come and help me.

MAGGIE. (*lifts* **ANNABEL** *the arm of the couch in sitting position*) What are we going to do with her?

JOEY. Make a suggestion. I don't do this every day, either.

MAGGIE. Let's sit her on something.

(**ANNABEL** *drops prone onto the couch.*)

Oops.

JOEY. Don't "oops" her! Be careful!

MAGGIE. I am. Don't be so touchy.

(**MAGGIE** *tries to lift her to the couch, but* **ANNABEL** *slips and lands on the floor in front of the couch.*)

MAGGIE. Oh, Lord, there she goes again.

JOEY. Tell me about it. She's got more moves than Michael Jackson.

MAGGIE. I thought you got stiff when you died. Let's *sit her up* on the couch.

JOEY. No way. Mom's as hairy as Midas about her being in here.

MAGGIE. Midas was not hairy. Or nervous. And I don't think Mom will mind. After all, it's Annabel. She just drank, she wasn't dirty.

JOEY. I never said she was dirty, just put her down.

MAGGIE. On the floor?

JOEY. What? You want to sit her up with a glass of lemonade?

MAGGIE. (**MAGGIE** *lowers* **ANNABEL** *to the floor.*) Lighten up. Don't get gross.

JOEY. *(composing himself)* I don't mean to be. Just…well, things get to you.

MAGGIE. It's not "things." And don't call it "something like this." It's death! She's dead, Joey. Get with the program.

JOEY. It's not a program. Like I was saying, "something like this" gets to you. Turns you around. You see different. I mean you can talk the talk about death and dying all you want, but it's not the same as holding Annabel's corpse in your arms.

MAGGIE. I hear that. *(pause)* Actually, I'm wondering if we can bring this off.

JOEY. *(sits on the floor)* You can't back out now. We have to finish. At least the one.

MAGGIE. *(joins* **JOEY** *on the floor)* I know. He promised Ed. We're hooked, now.

JOEY. You should have seen Ed's face when Dad said we'd do it for a thousand.

MAGGIE. A thousand? Can we do it for that?

JOEY. When Dad saw the shape Ed was in, crying and all, he whispered to me we ought to do things like this for free.

MAGGIE. We should have seen that coming. But, gracious, Joey. The coffin alone will cost that much.

JOEY. *(unsure)* Don't start a panic. We'll make the coffin.

MAGGIE. You think you can?

JOEY. You can do anything when there are no options. And there are none, Ed was crying, talking about how life was more than he could take anymore. How Annabel was a good girl that life turned on.

MAGGIE. *(looks at **ANNABEL**)* That must have torn you two up.

JOEY. It wasn't easy. But Dad told him we were all in it together and we would do what we could.

*(Long pause. Both are pensive, looking at **ANNABEL**.)*

I always liked Annabel.

MAGGIE. Me, too. There, but-for-fortune...you know.

JOEY. Exactly. And she was something else in her good old days. I mean gooooood looking.

MAGGIE. I thought you had a crush on her when we were little.

JOEY. Crush! I was dying. Once, oh, I must have been about twelve, I went up to the old Starland Drive-In and sneaked from car to car looking to see if she was there with someone.

MAGGIE. You didn't.

JOEY. Gospel. *(beat)* Do you remember Starland?

MAGGIE. Sure. You know they're selling that land now.

JOEY. Trying to.

(Both become lost in their thoughts and memories.)

MAGGIE. I walked up there last spring. It's so funny to see all those silent speakers where no one has seen or listened to a movie in years.

JOEY. Everything around here is haunted. Drive-in theaters. The old drug store. Closed schools.

MAGGIE. The boarded up stores and hollowed out churches. Empty playgrounds, Ghosts scurry everywhere around the old coal camps.

JOEY. And everything used to be so different. Even Annabel...

MAGGIE. I think, mostly the Annabels. They get smashed hardest when fallen dreams start falling.

JOEY. I reckon. You grow up. Figure to marry, have your kids. Work hard and buy your house. Nice lawn, white fence, and in the spring, a little garden with new lettuce and spring onions.

MAGGIE. And you save up all winter and once a summer go to Virginia Beach and –

(She stops mid-sentence; both are remembering summers at the beach.)

JOEY. Who thinks their towns can die?

MAGGIE. Do you think Annabel's life would have been different if she lived somewhere else?

JOEY. Who knows things like that?

MAGGIE. I was just remembering that big wedding when she and Bob got married.

JOEY. Mines were doing bonanza then. Then they shut down. Tom left. Bob got too desperate too fast and couldn't live with the fact he couldn't take care of Annabel.

MAGGIE. You believe that's why he left?

JOEY. I more than believe it. I understand it.

MAGGIE. Well, he was wrong. She may have had a chance with him. When he left was when Annabel's life slipped out of her reach. She got down and desperate and somebody bought her a drink.

JOEY. Then somebody bought a second one. Another somebody bought the next.

MAGGIE. The same somebodies who call her a drunk. And the only reason she drank was because her life didn't fit.

JOEY. *(smiles at the memory)* Do you remember when she worked at the Tic Toc?

MAGGIE. She'd give me extra French fries.

JOEY. Ha ha, me, too. One time I recited that Poe poem to her. *(gets down on one knee beside **ANNABEL**)*

"T'was many and many a year ago! In the kingdom by the sea!

That a maiden there lived, whom you know!

By the name of Annabel Lee."

And she put those hands on her hips and said… *(mimics)* "Why you, Joey Woolwine, what in hell's gone wrong in your silly head, I swear I think that little pea-dab of a brain of yours is done gone."

MAGGIE. *(fragile laugh)* I can hear her now.

(They sit, pensively, as lights fade.)

Scene Four

(Moments later. Lights rise on **MAGGIE** *and* **JOEY** *as* **BESS** *stomps into the room like a loose cannon.* **TOM** *is right behind her.)*

BESS. *(so upset, she doesn't notice* **ANNABEL***)* No, no, no, no, no!

TOM. Darn it, Bess, we have a situation here.

BESS. Absolutely, positively, and teetotallingly no. No, no!

TOM. Will you listen to reason for one minute'?

BESS. I can listen till the cows come home! I can listen till Jimmy Carter is reelected, but you are not bringing that body into my kitchen, nor using my table to do whatever it is you are going to do!

(crosses down to sit on the couch and almost stumbles over **ANNABEL***)*

Oh, my goodness, it's Annabel.

TOM. That's what I was trying to tell you.

BESS. *(kneels)* Annabel. I am so sorry. For everything. It's not that l don't want you here. *(catches herself)* Do you hear me? Do you hear me apologizing to a corpse? Do you hear me?

GRAN. *(following in from the kitchen, standing behind the couch)* We hear you. I dare say parts of Kentucky and Virginia and parts of Alabama hear you.

MAGGIE. Mom, chill, Now, I know this is a little inconvenient –

BESS. *(with amazement)* Inconvenient! Maggie, I'm not sure what I'd put past you anymore.

JOEY. Me, either. First thing you know, come some November, our Maggie might go out there and vote Republican.

*(***TOM** *and* **GRAN** *laugh.)*

TOM. *(stops abruptly)* Joey, what is she doing on the floor?

(**JOEY** *quickly tries to lift* **ANNABEL**. *The following statements are rapid as unease increases.*)

JOEY. I didn't mean disrespect. We just didn't know where to put her.

BESS. Can't you sit her up in a chair proper?

JOEY. I don't think she'll fold into a chair now. What about the couch?

BESS. Don't dare put her on my couch. *(embarrassed)* I mean, Gran may want to sit.

GRAN. I don't want to sit.

(**ANNABEL** *is stiff now;* **JOEY** *goes to her feet and pushes to get her legs to bend at the knee, but they keep straightening out.*)

JOEY. She won't go. She can't sit. Someone do something.

TOM. Just unfold her, Joey!

JOEY. She is unfolded, Dad. The trick is to fold her.

TOM. For crying out loud, put her in the recliner.

MAGGIE. *(near tears)* That seems ironic. Annabel worked her whole life.

JOEY. It's a recliner, Maggie. Surely you can imagine Annabel reclining.

(*Works with* **TOM** *and they carry her to the recliner. She is too stiff to sit, and doesn't conform to the chair until* **TOM** *reaches to lever it to the reclining position..*)

BESS. I won't allow such jokes. Tom, do you hear what's happening here now that we're in business?

TOM. All right, that is teetotallingy it! I don't want to hear another word. All of you! Get pit! We have work to do, so you get out and let me and Joey start. Now!

(**MAGGIE** *and* **BESS** *exit quickly.* **TOM** *and* **JOEY** *go into the kitchen and begin clearing off the table.* **GRAN** *goes to the porch, sits and rocks as the men get the table into the family room.* **JOEY** *looks at* **ANNABEL**. *Seeing his son's emotion,* **TOM** *is moved and goes back into the kitchen to pour himself a glass of water.* **GRAN** *comes to him.*)

GRAN. Son.

TOM. I'm all right, Mama. Go back on the porch.

GRAN. There's a chill out. *(beat)* It sets you thinking.

TOM. It does that. Thinking about everything. About how desperate things have gotten. Thinking how much you love your kids, and loving makes you holler at them. Thinking it's natural to want your kids with you, but if you love them, you ought to send them out of a dead place even if you call it home.

GRAN. Maybe you ought to go.

TOM. How? Where would I go? What can I do? Fifty-five, and no special skills when people with skills are out of work. *(pause, tries to make her feel better)* Besides, I love it here. Here is who I am, I love these mountains even when I wonder why the hell a man loves mountains.

GRAN. You sound scared.

TOM. Down to the insides of my bones. I have fear choking me. Fearing these old coal towns are emptying out of people. And knowing the smart and powerful ones who know how to make change are all gone, and those of us left aren't smart or powerful enough to fix things.

GRAN. I feel your feelings, boy, and I weep your grief, but you're wrong. You have smarts and power you haven't used yet.

TOM. *(smiles; hugs her)* I hope so, Mama, I sure hope so. Because you're hearing my innards talking. Oh, when the kids are around, I talk the talk so they don't get discouraged. But *(beat)* I'm afraid,

GRAN. And even so, you'll get the job done. You always do.

TOM. May be. *(starts toward family room)* But I have to tell you. Us trying this with Annabel has got me wondering how far will a person go when he's got nowhere to go?

(**GRAN** *follows and as* **TOM** *and* **JOEY** *begin preparations,* **GRAN** *talks to* **ANNABEL**.)

GRAN. *(Tenderly pushes back* **ANNABEL***'s hair.)* Annabel, I want to say how sorry I am about all this. Now, don't you take that as me saying I think you was living right, because I don't. Still and all, you were middling-young and a body cant help but wish life had turned out for you. But it didn't. So we got to go on going on, because that's what it's about, you know girl, all us Woolwines and Tollivers, all the good and sorry lot of us have to go on, and I'm hoping you understand what my boy's trying to do for you and yours. It's what your Pa would have done if he had thought of it, Now, you know we Woolwines will do the best we can by you, so, hang in there.

TOM. You're going to have to go, Mama.

GRAN. *(Rises to exit.)* Going. I just want you to know I can help without a blink of an eye.

JOEY. Go on, Gran. We're okay.

GRAN. No, you're not. You're all shook up. You youngens are so used to taking the sick over to Stevens Clinic to die by machinery instead of life, you don't know what dying looks like.

JOEY. There's some truth in that.

GRAN. Gospel. Best thing to do with death is look it right in the eye like folks have done since Day-One in Eden. Humph, you take a body to a hospital and plug it into all the I.V.'s and tubes, why, truth to tell, your Grandpa looked like a Sony those last days.

TOM. Just go.

GRAN. Going. But you're not much better than him, Thomas Lloyd. You look here at her, now. it's just Annabel.

JOEY. *(moved, mutters)* Annabel.

GRAN. And remember, she's up there in her realest home now and she don't care a kernel for what's here no more.

JOEY. I wonder if it's like that.

GRAN. Pure fact. Like Paul told, here's only a dim dark looking-glass, but Annabel sees clear with the brightest light that can be now.

TOM. Maybe. *(begins leading GRAN off)* Now, go ponder it.

GRAN. Don't have to. I got the shining. The knowing. *(She lets TOM lead her off, sings:)* "Tenderly. tenderly, Jesus is calling, calling for you and for me…"

(TOM takes GRAN off as she sings; he returns and he and JOEY stand looking at ANNABEL as lights fade.)

ACT TWO

Scene One

(Lights rise on **TOM** *and* **JOEY** *in the same position as at the end of Act One. Throughout this scene the tensions mount.)*

TOM. Let's get her on the table.

JOEY. She won't fit. She's about two feet longer than the table.

TOM. All I want you to do, Joey, is what I tell you to do.

JOEY. But, Dad –

TOM. I don't want to hear it!

(They struggle and get **ANNABEL** *on the table; her legs stick out at the bottom.* **JOEY** *shoves her body upward until her head is edging off the top.)*

JOEY. Like I said. Wrong size. It won't work.

TOM. It will work! *(bites words as* **MAGGIE** *enters)* Just! Do it!

MAGGIE. She's too long. I read somewhere that some undertakers actually cut off parts of the body to make it fit the coffin.

TOM. Too much! Don't even say it! Your mother's right, this business brings out the barbarian in you. Get out!

MAGGIE. No. I'm just telling you what I read. Now, if this is a family business, I can do my part.

JOEY. Give in, Dad, she's liberated. I saw her sneak in a Cosmopolitan magazine. And as far as this man's concerned, she can do it all.

MAGGIE. *(calculating)* What might work is if you put a section of the sofa under her thighs. That would keep her feet from dangling.

JOEY. Nothing about her dangles about now. She's as ramrod straight as can be, and I wouldn't touch Mom's couch for all the beer in Berlin.

TOM. It might work. Slip that section of couch under her, Joey.

(**JOEY** *gets section.* **MAGGIE** *and* **TOM** *lift* **ANNABEL**'s *legs and slip the section underneath.*)

JOEY. Eureka! She fits!

TOM. But her bottom's up. That can't be good.

MAGGIE. It could work for us. We need blood flow.

TOM. But is that where it should flow?

JOEY. That's life. As the blood flows.

(**BESS** *enters with a spray can.*)

MAGGIE. Mom, what are you doing?

BESS. *(spraying)* Nothing. I just thought of this.

TOM. *(grabs can)* Are you out of your ever-loving mind?

BESS. *(embarrassed)* What's wrong? I don't see anything wrong. It just dawned on me. Someone around here has to be practical.

JOEY. *(lifts* **ANNABEL**'s *arm)* Here, Mom, don't miss her underarms.

BESS. Do you hear him? If blasphemy is where this business leads, I'd prefer to be penniless.

TOM. We can't go on penniless. Now, go away.

BESS. Alright. *(grabs the can and sprays vigorously as she exits)*

TOM. Joey, get in the kitchen and get the stuff like I told you.

(**JOEY** *exits.*)

MAGGIE. Hang in there, Dad. She's just nervous and upset. Though she does seem to want to help.

TOM. And doing a bang-up job. I sure didn't think about body odor. *(looks at* **ANNABEL**) Maybe the second one will be easier.

(**JOEY** *returns, clanging an armload of drain guttering and a power drill.*)

Just drop it, and let's start rigging it up.

(**JOEY** and **TOM** *begin working out the guttering to make a long drain that will go into a bucket.*)

MAGGIE. Drain guttering? You can't use guttering.

JOEY. You have, maybe, real embalming equipment in your room?

MAGGIE. And is that a power drill?

TOM. Maggie, you listen up good! We have a problem here! This is not, *Third Rock from The Sun*. This is real, bona fide-crazy-reality!

MAGGIE. But what's with the power drill?

JOEY. To puncture her, what else? You know your Shakespeare, "If we prick her, she'll bleed." We need her to bleed, Maggie.

TOM. Cut it out, Joey.

JOEY. Do we have to cut things out, too?

MAGGIE. You can't do this. Pricking her is one thing. Puncturing her is another. You can't drill a hole in Annabel.

TOM. (*frustrated: to* **MAGGIE**) If I had time to sit and talk poetically about it, I would.

MAGGIE. But guttering, Dad.

TOM. Honey, we have to drain her.

JOEY. And K-Mart didn't have a beautiful, tasteful, velvet-covered – blood-drain for these occasions.

TOM. Joey, I want you to consider those your last words. You want to do a Rosie O'Donnell talk show, go to New York. Maggie, get out! Now, we have to prick her and prick her we will! I didn't know what to get for the job, and the best thought I had was this power drill. It seemed the best prick-device I could think of that wouldn't take a month of Mondays to drain. So we got the power drill. Now. Joey, do it.

JOEY. (*double take*) Joey do it?

(**TOM** *glares at* **JOEY** *and then starts fitting more guttering sections together.* **MAGGIE** *and* **JOEY** *help and the three continue working during the following.*)

MAGGIE. All right. But as soon as there is some money, we need to buy the proper equipment even before sending Joey to mortician classes.

TOM. Don't worry about it now. Now, concentrate on what's at hand. Go get the scrub bucket.

MAGGIE. Scrub bucket'?

JOEY. We have to catch all that blood. What do you want to use, champagne glasses?

(*The exchange becomes more rapid, more tense.*)

TOM. Joey, I'm begging.

MAGGIE. You can't drain Annabel into a scrub bucket!

JOEY. What worries me is a scrub bucket won't hold it all.

TOM. Think not?

JOEY. No. Ballpark figure, but I think a body has several buckets full.

TOM. Could be. Maggie, get the spaghetti pot, too.

MAGGIE. No way, Mom will have a teetotalling conniption fit.

JOEY. Gospel.

TOM. Just go get it. I'll get her a new one before we have spaghetti.

(**MAGGIE** *reluctantly goes to the kitchen to get the pot.* **JOEY** *and* **TOM** *work on fittings.*)

JOEY. Drains near finished. Should I plug in the drill?

TOM. Not yet. *(lifts book, reads)* I have to read a little farther to see what to do when we get the blood out.

JOEY. You put embalming fluid in at some point.

TOM. Thank you. I didn't know that. You are so helpful.

JOEY. It won't help to get touchy.

TOM. Touchy? Me? Naw, I'm thrilled to pieces to have these smart kids. Now, if you'll just tell me where to get the embalming fluid.

JOEY. I don't know.

TOM. You guess Mom keeps it in the fridge? No, no, maybe K-Mart carries it. Or, try Big Lots. Maybe we can save a few bucks.

JOEY. *(suppressing anger)* I just mentioned it. Only place I think may have it is a funeral home.

TOM. Well, there you go! What say you run over, casual-like, and ask Fred, like a neighbor, if we can borrow a gallon of embalming fluid, like it's sugar or cornflakes.

JOEY. Hold on, don't get crazy. You're the one with the book. Where did they get it in Ancient Egypt?

TOM. They didn't use embalming fluid. They used natron. Like I told you, they soaked the body. You want to go tell the Tollivers that we have to hold up the funeral because we're marinating Annabel?

MAGGIE. *(enters with pots and buckets)* Why the hollering?

JOEY. This isn't hollering. It's a professional discussion about technique.

TOM. Just put the spaghetti pot where the drain ends.

JOEY. *(seriously)* What about anti-freeze?

TOM. Anti-freeze? You think Annabel's in danger of freezing?

JOEY. Will everyone chill! I don't know what embalming fluid is. I'm just trying to think of something it might be like. Cripes! I'm just trying.

TOM. Try harder, Joey, try harder.

MAGGIE. You two are way too tense. Now, I hate to say anything.

TOM. Then don't. There's enough talk going on here to start our own congress. Now, Joey, lift the sheet and start.

JOEY. What's with this business, "Joey, lift the sheets?"

TOM. It means, lift the sheets. You expect maybe fairies to come tonight and do it?

JOEY. *(hesitantly touches the tip of the sheet, drops it)* I can't. I'm sorry, Dad. I just can't.

MAGGIE. He had a crush on her, Dad.

TOM. I don't care if they were secretly married. He finishes what he starts.

(Suddenly realizes his tension and JOEY's pain, etc., draws a deep breath.)

It's all right, son. I just wish you'd said something.

JOEY. I didn't want to let you down.

MAGGIE. I can help.

(MAGGIE gets power drill and hands it to TOM who takes it, snaps it on, and begins looking up and down ANNABEL's body.)

Do you want me to do it?

TOM. I do not! Right now I'm wishing kids came from factories so you could return them when they prove defective.

(JOEY is amused at the remark; MAGGIE is hurt.)

MAGGIE. That's not fair.

TOM. And I don't mean it. Just one of you, please, tell me where to start Annabel.

MAGGIE. *(gets book)* Would it be in here?

JOEY. I doubt they used a power drill in ancient Egypt.

MAGGIE. Funny. But they must have gotten the blood out. How?

JOEY. All I remember from history class was they took out vital organs and put them in canopic jars.

TOM. And I'm pretty sure Mom threw out our canopic jars.

MAGGIE. Seriously, though, ou have to think of Annabel's appearance. You can't put a hole in her where it would show.

JOEY. Under her arms might be a good place.

TOM. I hate to mess with her arms. Ed wants her to wear that sleeveless blue taffeta dress she wore to the prom.

JOEY. I just hope we can get it all out with one hole. I'd hate a bunch of holes in her.

MAGGIE. Especially not on her arms. People will start talking the talk, and one thing about Annabel, she would not do drugs.

JOEY. Right. Annabel said no to drugs. I think Nancy Reagan would have liked Annabel.

TOM. Underarms it is.

(lifts **ANNABEL***'s arm, turns on drill)*

MAGGIE. Start it. What are you waiting for?

TOM. I am, I am. *(snaps off drill; puts the arm down)* Make sure the drain's in place.

MAGGIE. The drain is in place.

TOM. All the joints fitted together tight.

JOEY. Like drums. You go, Dad.

TOM. Here goes. *(lifts drill high, turns it on)*

TONI. *(off)* Mr. Woolwine. Yoo hoo, Mr. Woolwine.

(All freeze. **TOM** *has the drill lifted in the air and it stays on during their panic.)*

JOEY. Who in God's green acres can it be?!

TOM. *(arm with drill still in the air)* Stay cool. Stay calm and cool. No one get upset.

TONI. *(still off)* Yoo hoo, Mr. Woolwine.

JOEY. Dad, it's someone. Turn off the drill.

TOM. It's no one. It can't be somebody. I'll turn off the drill. *(turns it off)* It can't be someone. That's impossible.

TONI. *(peeking around the edge of the door she partially opened)* Hi there, Mr. Woolwine, didn't you hear me?

JOEY. Here comes the impossible right at us.

TOM. Shut up! And cover Annabel!

*(***JOEY*** and* **MAGGIE** *quickly throw a sheet over* **ANNABEL** *and try unsuccessfully to sit a vase on her so it will appear an ordinary table; the vase topples as* **TONI** *reaches the stage.)*

TONI. Is anyone home?

TOM. *(steps in front of table)* Just us.

(**JOEY** *puts the vase on the floor, leans casually against the table as* **TONI** *brings over her briefcase and small tape recorder.*)

TONI. *(effervescently friendly, extends hand)* Mr. Woolwine, I presume?

(**ANNABEL**'s *arm falls from under the covers:* **MAGGIE** *hurriedly covers it.*)

TOM. Well, hi there. Boy, this is an unexplained – that is, unexpected pleasure.

TONI. *(motor-mouth – sales pitch.)* My name is Cassandra Antoinette Withholden, but everyone calls me "Little Toni" because my father's name is Tony, too. And you can just imagine the Withholden jokes. Like "what-am-I-withholden?" It's an old English name.

JOEY. That is interesting.

TONI. *(takes him seriously)* Names can be. When I heard yours was Woolwine, I thought, somewhere, long, long, in their past, their ancestors were in the wool and wine business. That's how names start. Did you know that your progenitors were in wool and wine?

JOEY. I don't doubt it? And, your progenitors?

TOM. *(overwhelmed)* Don't joke, Joey.

TONI. No problem. He's just teasing. Mountain humor. I just love Appalachia. I told the central office, let me go, I just love West Virginians. I'm like one of you. My family used to come to White Sulphur Springs when I was young, so I'm almost a native. I love all those quilts. *(to* **MAGGIE***)* Do you quilt?

MAGGIE. No. I never.

TONI. *(thrusts hand to* **MAGGIE***)* And your name?

MAGGIE. Maggie. He's Joey.

TONI. *(shakes* **MAGGIE***'s hand vigorously, then* **JOEY***'s)* Maggie, what a perfectly perfect mountain name, but you don't quilt?

MAGGIE. I'm sorry.

JOEY. *(angered, speaks in a caricature of mountain drawl)* She used to quilt, Ma'am, but she took ta readin' Playgirl, and first thing you know, she's out burnin' quilts.

TOM. Joey, chill. He doesn't mean anything offensive.

JOEY. Yes, I do. Who the hell are you, lady?

TONI. You mean, you really don't know?

JOEY. No. We don't know. We have no idea. We can't imagine.

TONI. Well, I'm pissed! Central Office will hear about this. You should have been notified.

(The Woolwines start to panic, assuming she's the law.)

TOM. Central Office?

MAGGIE. Notify us?

TONI. This really scalds me. You do know I'm here about this new business you've started.

TOM. *(stretches arms in front of table as* **ANNABEL***'s arm falls out again)* New business?

TONI. *(tries to set briefcase on table, it topples)* Central Office got a call about you.

MAGGIE. Already? We're only starting today?

TONI. *(starts to straighten briefcase)* We work hard. You have opened a new enterprise, haven't you?

TOM. I think "open" is a little misleading at this point.

TONI. *(struggles to straighten briefcase in the body throughout)* You have taken the first steps.

JOEY. "First steps" is a little much.

TONI. But we heard you were accepting customers.

MAGGIE. *(whispers to* **TOM***)* Oh. Lord, Dad it is the government.

TOM. What government?

JOEY. Probably not Japan. Better find something to tell her.

TOM. Right. Ah. Listen, Ms. Withholden –

TONI. Just Toni –

TOM. Okay, Toni. Thing is we didn't mean to start any trouble. You don't know what its like around here with the mines closed, and I guess this seems sort of crazy... Well. It is sort of crazy. But the truth is, we haven't even started yet.

TONI. I see. You're at the drawing board stage.

TOM. Not even drawing board, just, ha ha, kitchen table, for now.

MAGGIE. But we mean to get world-class-Grade-A government inspected equipment as soon as we can, and you can tell the government that.

TONI. Tell which government what?

MAGGIE. Just say it, Ms. Withholden. We know you're with some inspection system or other. You said you got a call about us.

JOEY. Though for the life of me, I never heard of West Virginia working this fast on anything.

(**TONI** *gets a microphone from the briefcase, attaches it to the tape recorder and lays it on* **ANNABEL** *as both her arms flop out.*)

TONI. *(chirpy)* Okay, let's get started.

JOEY. *(responds to the mic)* Okay, all right, we'll cooperate.

MAGGIE. We'll stop, in fact. You don't have to record us.

TONI. Record you? You're kidding. Now, I need an outlet. I'm afraid my batteries are dead.

JOEY. Mine are dying. *(indicates)* And there's an outlet.

TONI. *(plugs in recorder)* Good. No, I'm not recording. I'll just ask you to listen for a moment. *(recorder slips off* **ANNABEL**.*)* What kind of cockamamie table is this?

JOEY. Just a typical table.

MAGGIE. Of course, it's typical, what are you implying? *(shoves one of* **ANNABEL**'s *arms under covers)* Well, I guess not typical, as tables go...it's made with chestnuts.

TOM. Yeah, chestnuts. See, my wife's great grandfather was something of an artist and he made this table. *(pats* **ANNABEL***)* Yes, sir, he glued little chestnuts all over it and that explains the lumps.

TONI. They don't look like chestnut lumps.

JOEY. You know, you're just real suspicious, Toni. And, I for one, am real tired of it. Now, if you're not from the government, who are you and why are you hasseling us?

TONI. I am not. But, I'm forgetting you don't know. I'm from the Pythagorean Music Company.

MAGGIE. *(sarcasm)* Now it's real clear.

TOM. Toni, I'm not a rude man, but believe me, these are rude times for me. I'm about as busy as a man gets, and I never heard of your pythy company.

TONI. Exactly. I told them no one would know that name. It was an ancient Greek philosopher who thought we heard perfect music on a prior plane.

JOEY. I can understand that. Obviously not Delta.

MAGGIE. Good Lord, she's selling canned music.

TONI. *(gets huffy)* I think "canned music" is a little banal. We have the latest in a variety of surprisingly melodious and hauntingly harmonious melodies for your most discerning customers.

JOEY. *(relieved)* Annabel only listened to Elvis.

TONI. *(hits tape button; samba music; dances as she talks)* – And there are those who prefer new sounds in funeral music, something a bit more upbeat with a good sound and movement to it. or…*(Fast-forwards tape to folk music.)* Or, your client might prefer some old mountainy, folksy whatever. Actually, people don't want to think death music all that much, and, of course, nothing reminds you of death so much as having someone you know laying there dead in front of you all evening.

JOEY. That does it for me.

TONI. – So, get rid of that, you know, lose the draggy "death-lag" funeral music and… *(Fast-forwards to rock music; dances.)* …Why not rock?

TOM. I'd want to be polite, but we're flat-broke-busted.

TONI. *(desperate)* You don't understand how cheap we are! *(Turns volume down.)* You'll freak when you hear our incredible price. You won't believe what I'm about to tell you.

JOEY. I can't believe any of this, so far.

TONI. I'm talking everything, now, mind you. Wiring, installation and piping all these paradisiacal sounds in your parlor. I'm talking discs and the best damn technical equipment we and the Japanese can put together.

TOM. Toni, ARE YOU NOT LISTENING TO ME?!

TONI. But you've not heard everything.

MAGGIE. I think he has.

TONI. I'm about to end all reservations by quoting you the unbelievable low-spring-sale price of only eight thousand, nine-hundred and ninety dollars. *(beat)* If you buy by June first.

TOM. *(becomes uncharacteristically violent; yanks the cord from the outlet and wraps it around **TONI**.)* Throw her out!

MAGGIE. Dad?

TOM. Out, out, out! Joey, if you don't do it quickly I'll hurt you.

TONI. Tom, you're such a joker.

TOM. Throw her out the door, down the steps and onto the street.

(**JOEY** *starts dragging her out.*)

TONI. *(shouts over her shoulder as she's dragged off)* You don't understand how this can work. They call, you're busy, so you put them on hold and our system says, "Thank you for calling the Palace of Heavenly Rest. Our Lines are busy –" Then the music starts, "Oh, when the saints, go marching in, oh when the saints – "

(*As* **TONI***'s voice trails off a door slams and* **TOM** *slumps to the sofa, defeated.*)

MAGGIE. Hey, she's no reason to get discouraged. Though, I admit, your, "Throw her out!" sort of threw me. *(sits next to him, puts arm around his shoulder)* Don't beat yourself up. She asked for it.

TOM. No, she didn't, hons. She's just trying to make a buck, like us. Ha, me, Conan the Barbarian, huh?

JOEY. *(returns, hands a pamphlet to* **TOM***)* She left these ads for when you come to your senses.

TOM. Wonder when that will be?

JOEY. She sort of got to me.

MAGGIE. Are you kidding?

JOEY. No. Turns out she's not from some big company. She and her husband bought the one sound system and got to see if they could turn a couple of bucks selling them to funeral homes.

MAGGIE. Sold many?

JOEY. Not as many as we've done bodies. But, hey, can we call the kettle incredible?

TOM. Makes you wonder how far a person will go – *(doesn't finish)* Whatever. But she did me a good turn.

JOEY. How so?

TOM. Her being here gave me time to think.

JOEY. While she was speed-talking?

TOM. Yeah. Having someone show up made me realize how this looks. Seeing it by real light. Here I was worrying about hurting Annabel and that's not the problem. We can't hurt her. It just goes to show we're not called to do this.

MAGGIE. True or not, we have to do this one. *(voice breaking)* We just have to be gentle.

JOEY. It's hard to be gentle with a power drill. *(Pause; looks at each of them.)* Yeah, we have to. We promised.

TOM. Right. I'm just realizing that if it feels this wrong, it must not be ours to do. We're miners, and it seems to me that God gives all a call and if this was ours, we'd feel okay. But, I promised Ed, so we have to do what we have to do. *(Lifts drill. Turns it on as lights fade.)*

Scene Two

(Lights rise on empty family room as **MAGGIE** *is heard singing offstage.)*

MAGGIE. *(offstage, sings)* "Now the day is over, Night is drawing nigh. Shadows of the evening. Steal across the sky."

*(***BESS*** enters living room from down right, and stands listening.)*

"Jesus give the wary, Calm and sweet repose. In thy tender mercies, May our eyelids close."

GRAN. *(enters; stands behind* **BESS**.*)* Bessie-girl, are you all right?

BESS. Yes, Gran

GRAN. Still feels funny having a wake right there in your dining room.

BESS. In a way. But you're right about how "things used to be." It feels right, too, somehow.

*(***MAGGIE*** enters from kitchen crossing into family room to* **GRAN**.*)*

And speaking of doing the right thing, honey, your singing was beautiful.

MAGGIE. I hope so. We're so edgy, having Annabel here and all.

BESS. I was just saying how good it seemed.

MAGGIE. We did our best.

BESS. And your best was wonderful. I'm proud of you. And I've been such a pain in the butt.

MAGGIE. *(uneasy, but smiles, kisses* **BESS** *on the cheek)* Somebody has to do it.

GRAN. Well, it was hard, and you did fine. Everyone is impressed.

BESS. Annabel looks so sweet. You three can take pride in a job well done.

MAGGIE. Don't say that.

BESS. Don't be modest. She's lovely.

MAGGIE. Don't. You always caution that pride goes before a fall.

(TOM enters, stands back awkwardly, uncomfortable.)

GRAN. It was perfect, Maggie. No angel will sing prettier than you on the other side.

MAGGIE. I hope you're wrong. I'm counting on better celestial music. *(nods to TOM)* Pythagorean, in fact.

BESS. What?

MAGGIE. *(trying to ease TOM's tensions)* Inside undertaker's joke, Mom.

TOM. It seems to be going pretty good in there.

BESS. Good? Better than I dreamed.

TOM. Don't overdo.

BESS. I'm under-doing. I have to admit I didn't think you could actually go through with it, but you did as fine a job as I've ever seen.

TOM. Please, don't say that.

BESS. You three can act humble if you want, but I know you know how good Annabel looks. I'll say it from the rooftops, the Woolwines are great undertakers.

TOM. Hush the nonsense, Bess.

BESS. Why I'll shout it. You've made a believer of me.

GRAN. *(hesitant to speak, growing suspicious)* It's true, son. The Tollivers are that pleased. I'm not a braggart, *(watches him closely, fishing for truth)* but that looks like a professional job.

TOM. *(confirms GRAN's suspicions)* I wish you'd stop. Please, Mama.

BESS. I, frankly, don't know how you went through with it. And that casket! I don't know how you could swing that with the price you quoted Ed. I've never seen finer.

TOM. It's not that great. We see what we need to see.

(MAYOR PRICE enters.)

BESS. I assumed you got a bargain from Fred.

PRICE. Tom, I have to talk to you.

TOM. Being mayor, Bill, I sort of thought you would. *(pause)* I want to talk to you, too.

PRICE. I'm not here as mayor but as a friend. Yes sir, friend both to this family and the Tollivers, so don't go saying something that could land us in the new McDowell County Prison. First, I want to compliment you. *(puts up a hand to stop* **TOM***'s comment)* No, no, don't say anything. I understand what you wanted to do, start up a business and help others around here. I commend you. I see your point, and Ed's too. Thing is, I understand too, too well and I can do too, too little. I'm a limited man.

BESS. Don't be so modest, Bill. You're as good a man as Huntington or Charleston has.

PRICE. I'll take that for a little more compliment than it's actually worth, Bess. But the point is, Tom, you can't do this!

TOM. That's what I'm trying to tell you, Bill.

PRICE. Don't tell me anything! Less said, the better. I just can't let what you've done get it. It'd be like trying to stop gossip leaving a Kathy's beauty shop.

TOM. I'm trying to explain.

PRICE. Don't you know the advantage of your not telling me everything? Now, I got nothing but good to say about the job you did on Annabel. And I appreciate the money-break you gave the Tollivers, though for the life of me, I can't see how you did it for a thousand.

BESS. A thousand?

PRICE. Can you believe it? That fine coffin. I can't believe you did it for that price.

TOM. *(barely audible)* I didn't.

PRICE. *(doesn't understand)* That's what I thought. Figured the casket alone –

TOM. *(interrupts)* Yeah, the casket alone cost more than that. We'd figured to make a pine one, hurry-up-quick, but it didn't happen. And no, Bessie, we didn't get a bargain from Fred.

BESS. Do you mean to tell me that you bought that casket outright?

TOM. I sure don't mean to tell you.

BESS. No, Tom, I can't hear this. If you bought it, we have to be in debt. And we can't ask the Tollivers to help because you did it without asking them. Please say you didn't go buy a casket like that out right.

TOM. I did not go out and buy a casket out right.

BESS. I can't even guess what you mean.

GRAN. I can.

PRICE. Well, someone explain to me, as there's every chance I'll be explaining it to the authorities.

TOM. No, you won't. There's nothing to explain.

GRAN. I knew it.

PRICE. I don't. Here you go embalming, preparing a body without a license –

MAGGIE. We did not. We took Annabel over to Welch.

BESS. No.

MAGGIE. It'll take Dad a month of Mondays to get it out. We took her to a real funeral home and had her done.

PRICE. By professionals?

TOM. No, Bill, by amateurs like us. *(looks at BESS)* Sorry, hons.

BESS. But, you had to buy top-dollar.

TOM. Yep. *(emphatically)* And let's get it straight, this is our bill, not the Tolliver's. It's not what they agreed to. They don't know. and they're not going to know. They got a promise of a thousand-dollar funeral from me and that's what they pay. You got that, Bill? Because my family knows to listen when I make a promise like that.

PRICE. How can you pay for this?

TOM. Let me worry my worries.

BESS. I'm scared.

TOM. Bess. I can't tell you how sorry I am, but you know I had to do it. It was Ed's time of grieving and –

PRICE. I'd better get. You folks need to talk. *(exiting)* And I heard you, Tom, loud and clear. I'll not tell a soul. You worry our worries. *(exits)*

BESS. How much?

TOM. Well, if you total it all up, and add, like, the hearse we hired and, well, first, I guess about five thousand, but then, if you factor in –

MAGGIE. Eight thousand, Mom. Closer to nine.

BESS. *(breathless)* Oh, my goodness! That will take all our lives to pay.

MAGGIE. Remember, Mom, we'll have the thousand from the Tollivers.

BESS. *(realizing how hard they are all trying)* You're right, darling. There's that.

TOM. Honey, I can't begin to apologize for failing to do this.

BESS. Tom, don't –

TOM. But I need you to understand –

BESS. *(near tears)* What I understand is what a royal rear-end I've been. I'm ashamed enough of myself right now. *(smiles)* Crazy as this is, you all did your best to do something, while all I did was whine.

TOM. That's not true.

MAGGIE. Yes, it is. *(hugs BESS)* But someone has to do it.

BESS. The thing now is to figure out what we do next.

MAGGIE. I don't guess we could ask the Tollivers to at least go halves with us.

BESS. Of course not. Funeral arrangements are private, and we don't know what they might have selected. No, we just have to get those old mountain-thinking-caps back on, huh, Gran?

GRAN. Don't ask me. I think I've done enough.

BESS. You can't get away with self-pity, that's my act. Now, let's have another idea from someone.

TOM. *(looks away from GRAN)* Actually, I already have one.

GRAN. *(suppressing tears)* You have to do what you have to do.

TOM. *(looks into **GRAN**'s eyes)* That's why Joey's not at the wake. He's in Danville. He went to see if Jimmy's factory is hiring

(lights dim)

Scene Three

*(Two days later. Spot rises on luggage in the living room. A dim light is on **GRAN** rocking on the porch. **JOEY** comes up on the porch, looks silently at **GRAN**, then goes into the kitchen, picks up the forsythia which is beginning to bloom, and is looking at them when **TOM**, **BESS** and **MAGGIE** enter. **TOM** stands looking through the screen door at **GRAN** on the porch.)*

JOEY. Is everyone ready?

MAGGIE. As ready as were going to get.

BESS. Ready and rarin'. Gran fixed a big breakfast. Are you hungry?

JOEY. No. Diane cooked one, too. She's waiting in the car. She can hardly wait.

TOM. Then there's nothing stopping us / Let's go.

(All get luggage and return to kitchen.)

JOEY. *(nods toward porch)* You couldn't talk her into it.

BESS. I never thought for a minute we could.

TOM. Yeah, but then, I never thought I'd go.

BESS. She'll be fine. This is temporary.

MAGGIE. Gospel.

JOEY. And we all know Gran has the grits that gets.

(All make an effort at laughter.)

BESS. As soon as things pick up, we're back here. We'll get these hillbilly buns back where they belong.

TOM. Gospel. *(winks at **MAGGIE**)* Say those jobs begin Monday?

JOEY. Eight o'clock sharp. We're working men again. Me, you and Maggie.

MAGGIE. I won't bother with that sexism, Joey.

TOM. We got those jobs hurry up-quick. I didn't know your brothers had such pull in the brassiere factories of America.

JOEY. Well, they do. Jimmy said it only took him two years to get assistant *production* manager. It could happen to me. *(beat)* Virginia's full of West Virginians.

TOM. Yeah. So is North Carolina. South Carolina. Chicago. Detroit. Everywhere seems to have more West Virginians than West Virginia. We're just a state getting empty on itself.

BESS. But there's change coming. I feel it.

(The following lines are rapid, between bravado and belief.)

MAGGIE. *(smiles)* Could get to be gospel.

BESS. *(joins in)* Something has to do it.

TOM. But, good Lord. brassieres!

MAGGIE. Dare I say it'?

JOEY. Let me. Dirty work, but – (**MAGGIE** *says with him.*) Somebody has to do it.

MAGGIE. And think, Dad, you could make one that would end up on Dolly Parton.

TOM. Ha. Reckon they'd pay overtime for one of those.

BESS. Sounds like you all are really getting into this. *(pause)* But, we're stalling.

TOM. Yeah. Let's get this over with.

*(**TOM** hurriedly picks up the luggage and rushes off the porch only nodding to **GRAN**. The others come out more slowly and embrace her as they exit. After all exit, **GRAN** sits rocking as sounds of car doors slamming and the engine are heard. Then the car motor is turned off Another door slams and **TOM** runs up to **GRAN** kneels, takes her hand, turns it over and kisses the palm, then runs back off. The door slams again, the motor starts, and the car sounds fade, driving off in the distance] **GRAN** rocks a moment, then goes into the kitchen, gets the forsythia, arranges it and begins to sing "Farther Along" as lights fade.)*

The End

Suggested Set design

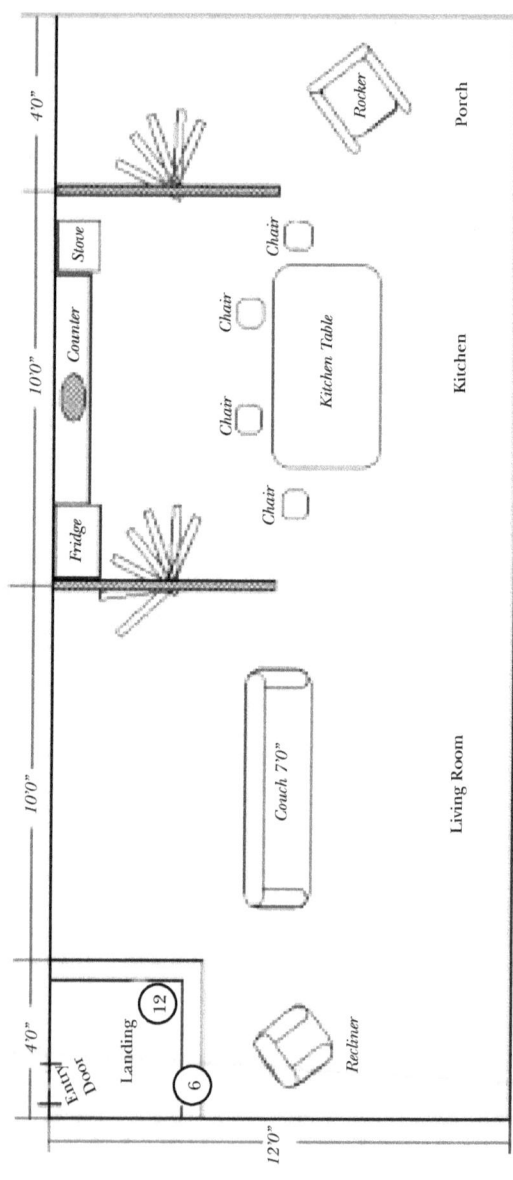

OTHER TITLES AVAILABLE FROM BAKER'S PLAYS

MOUNTAINS IN MY STRIDE

James Facos

Drama / 7m, 3w, + Extras

Mountains In My Stride is an indelibly American folk play, woven of mythic material, of people caught in the timeless trials of becoming their truest selves – whether in 1830 Missouri or now – facing head-on the need for courage, insight and inspiration to conquer their challenges. Jason Hunt, a veteran frontiersman, slated for Congress, finds his true destiny blocked by his love for Ruth, a young, wavering Bostonian, who demands security outside herself; while Hannah, her cousin must shatter the bonds of tradition if she is to find her real self – and true love. Blunder, raised by the Pawnee and now snared by the mercenary Sary, startles to find himself through his own native-wrought vision, which untangles all their lives.

Beautifully written, *Mountains In My Stride* is charged with true, dimensional characters, resonant themes, and a victorious spirit as one by one they take – or miss – the mountains in their lives.

BAKERSPLAYS.COM

OTHER TITLES AVAILABLE FROM BAKER'S PLAYS

MOUNTAINS IN MY STRIDE

Pat Cook

Drama / 4m, 6f / Interior

Ever look at a family portrait and wonder what those people, posed and smiling, are really like? This family portrait shows you the inner workings of the Rogers family – how they deal with everyday things, how they deal with both happy and sad events which effect each and every one of them. These funny, poignant and all-too-human characters go through life the best way they know how. Austin does his best to keep the house running smoothly, unless he has to take Pawpaw's trunk out of the basement. Mary Jo is outwardly pleased when son Mitchell gets engaged to Tish but explains "They're too young!" Her sister, Brenda, helps out by saying "Not any younger than you were when you got married." Brenda's husband, Dale, has his own advice for young Mitchell – "Marriage consists in large part of just giving up!" And Pawpaw keeps hearing voices and seeing people who aren't there. The very fabric of the family unit meets it's ultimate challenge when Brenda and Dale have to move in with them. Daughter Jan has to put up with a whiney dog, Mitchell and Tish can't seem to find time to talk about their upcoming marriage and everyone is bunking up with everyone else, leaving the men to sleep on the couch – any of this sound familiar? Brought to you by the same author of *Good Help is So Hard to Murder*.

BAKERSPLAYS.COM

www.ingramcontent.com/pod-product-compliance
Lightning Source LLC
Chambersburg PA
CBHW071843290426
44109CB00017B/1906